I move like this

Bobbie Kalman

 Crabtree Publishing Company

www.crabtreebooks.com

Created by Bobbie Kalman

Author and Editor-in-Chief
Bobbie Kalman

Educational consultants
Elaine Hurst
Joan King
Reagan Miller

Editors
Joan King
Reagan Miller
Kathy Middleton

Proofreader
Crystal Sikkens

Design
Bobbie Kalman
Katherine Berti

Production coordinator
Katherine Berti

Prepress technician
Katherine Berti

Photo research
Bobbie Kalman

Photographs and illustrations
BigStockPhoto: p. 6
Bonna Rouse: p. 8 (illustration)
All other photographs by Shutterstock

Library and Archives Canada Cataloguing in Publication

Kalman, Bobbie, 1947-
   I move like this / Bobbie Kalman.

(My world)
ISBN 978-0-7787-9429-5 (bound).--ISBN 978-0-7787-9473-8 (pbk.)

   1. Human locomotion--Juvenile literature.
I. Title. II. Series: My world (St. Catharines, Ont.)

QP301.K343 2010   j612.7'6   C2009-906060-4

Library of Congress Cataloging-in-Publication Data

Kalman, Bobbie.
   I move like this / Bobbie Kalman.
      p. cm. -- (My world)
   ISBN 978-0-7787-9473-8 (pbk. : alk. paper) -- ISBN 978-0-7787-9429-5
(reinforced library binding : alk. paper)
   1. Human locomotion--Juvenile literature. I. Title. II. Series.

   QP301.K 28 2010
   612.7'6--dc22
                                                                    2009040961

Crabtree Publishing Company

Printed in China/122009/CT20091009

www.crabtreebooks.com   1-800-387-7650

Published in Canada
Crabtree Publishing
616 Welland Ave.
St. Catharines, Ontario
L2M 5V6

Published in the United States
Crabtree Publishing
PMB 59051
350 Fifth Avenue, 59th Floor
New York, New York 10118

Published in the United Kingdom
Crabtree Publishing
Maritime House
Basin Road North, Hove
BN41 1WR

Published in Australia
Crabtree Publishing
386 Mt. Alexander Rd.
Ascot Vale (Melbourne)
VIC 3032

Words to know

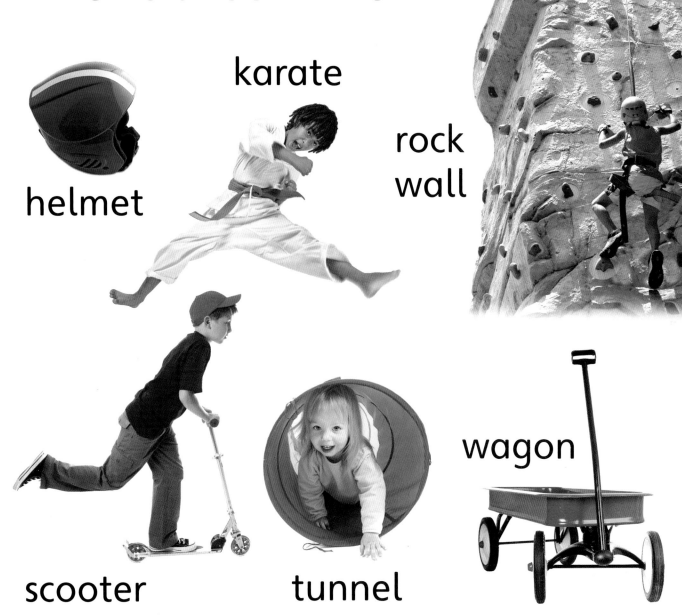

helmet

karate

rock wall

scooter

tunnel

wagon

3

I move like this
when I do karate.
I kick my legs **high**.
I punch with my fists.

I am hanging **upside down**.
I am hanging from the bars
by my hands and knees.

Our dog is walking
between my brother and me.
We go for a walk every day.

I am running **in front** of my dog.
My dog is running **behind** me.
We like to run **beside** the water.

I am jumping **over** my brother.
My brother is **under** me.
We are playing leapfrog.

I am sitting **inside** a basket.

My legs are hanging **outside** it.

"Help! Get me out!"

I am sitting **in** a wagon
with my dog.
My other dog is pulling
the wagon **forward**.

I am riding
on my scooter.
When I push
my leg **backward**,
my scooter
moves forward.

I am climbing **through** a tunnel.
The tunnel is **around** me.

I am climbing **up** a rock wall.
I wear a helmet to keep me safe.

Activity

Which child is hanging her head between her arms?

Which child is sitting on a swing?

Which child is bouncing up and down?

Which child is jumping into water?

Notes for adults

Moving and direction

Ask the children to list all the ways they have moved since they got up in the morning. Which body parts did they use for each movement? In which direction did they move? Ask them to use as many directional words as possible.

How do they move?

Why do we move? Are children aware that they are living things, and that living things move? How do other living things move? Ask the children to name different kinds of animals, such as fish, lizards, birds, snakes, cats, and frogs, and describe how they move. Have the children pretend to be different animals that move in different ways. They could choose to be birds, frogs, monkeys, elephants, horses, and so on. Children can hold an animal parade at home, around the classroom, or in the hallway of the school.

Where is it? is an award-winning book that teaches children about directions such as left and right, on and under, near and far, and many more.
Guided Reading: I

Find fascinating pictures and information about how animals move in ***How does it move?***
Guided Reading: I

16